# Linux for Beginners

## - 2nd Edition -

## *An Complete Introduction to the Linux Operating System and Command Line*

## M.J. Brown

# Linux for Beginners

# Disclaimer

This document is geared towards providing exact and reliable information in regards to the topic and issue covered. The publication is sold with the idea that the publisher is not required to render accounting, officially permitted, or otherwise, qualified services. If advice is necessary, legal or professional, a practiced individual in the profession should be ordered.

- From a Declaration of Principles which was accepted and approved equally by a Committee of the American Bar Association and a Committee of Publishers and Associations.

The information provided herein is stated to be truthful and consistent, in that any liability, in terms of inattention or otherwise, by any usage or abuse of any policies, processes, or directions contained within is the solitary and utter responsibility of the recipient reader. Under no circumstances will any legal responsibility or blame be held against the publisher for any reparation, damages, or monetary loss due to the information herein, either directly or indirectly.

The information herein is offered for informational purposes solely, and is universal as so. The presentation of the information is without contract or any type of guarantee assurance.

# Table of Contents

# Introduction

I want to thank you and congratulate you for buying the book, *"Linux for Beginners: An Introduction to the Linux Operating System and Command Line"*.

This book contains proven steps and strategies on how to start using Linux Operating System and Command line easily and seamlessly.

Modern computing is very different from old style computing. In fact, most of us probably wouldn't operate their PC without using the mouse and a nice GUI where we can simply click on whatever we want. Linux brings out the power of commands in the same way as the very first computers functioned. The only challenge is how to actually start using Linux when you have never used it, given that it seems to be simple to those who actually know it, but a totally new world to those who don't.

This doesn't mean that you are destined to continued use of Windows and other easy-to-use operating systems that don't give you the flexibility of doing whatever you want with your PC. This book seeks to introduce you to the new world of using Linux to do literally anything you would want to do. By reading this book, you will discover:

- How Linux came into being and how to start using it

- How to use some of the most common Linux commands

- How to use text editors

- How to use Linux on your Mac or Windows PC

- Everything about SSH including how to create SSH keys

- How to create, move, rename and move directories

- How to schedule and automate tasks using chron

- How to locate files, programs, documentation and configuration

# Linux for Beginners

- How you can access a Linux server

- Choosing the right distro

- Pipes and how to use them well

 And much, much more! It may appear to be a mystery at this time, but once you learn this language, you will be very pleased you did.


M.J. Brown

# Background

C omputer Operating systems are complicated for the majority of those who are not tech-savvy. Learning them can be a daunting task even for someone with a Master's Degree in Computer Science. Fortunately, I am here to help you navigate these murky waters. I have been a power computer user since the introduction of this technology. Over the years, I have watched as operating systems have come and go. Some have stood the test of time while others have not been so successful. Fortunately, I can make it to the list of the lucky few individuals who have had the opportunity to try out some of these computer operating systems, both those which have failed and those which have gone on to be big players in the personal computer industry. Among the many OSs I have had the pleasure and perhaps honor of testing and scrutinizing is LINUX, the UNIX based operating system.

As a software developer and all round tech freak, I have found Linux to be one of the most versatile and flexible operating systems in existence today. Here is the kicker though; you do not need to be a computer geek, nerd, or genius to enjoy the flexibility and power that Linux accords you as a user. All you need is that which drove Einstein to achieving, that which drove the Wright brothers to inventing, and that which led Galileo to discovering. That means having a thirst for knowledge.

It is my hope that, by the time you put down this book, you will look back and reflect on the journey we have been on with a new, informed, and anxious-to-get-started mindset and will be well on your way to becoming a power user. Let us start by examining Linux in its basic state.

# Linux for Dummies
## - An introduction to Linux -

U NIX, the "mother ship" to the Linux operating system, is not unlike a continuous flow of hot magma. In other words, it's evolving. Since its development in the 1960s, it has undergone drastic changes that have made it a favorite of most developers, both for software and mobile applications. Perhaps this is due to its open source nature. Firstly, it is not right for me to assume that you know what an operating system is. Therefore, here's an explanation. An operating system is the suite of programs behind the workings of your personal or work computer. There is a raging debate in the tech world as to whether there is a difference between Linux and UNIX; to be honest with you, I am not very sure if there is much difference between the two.

Linux, or UNIX, is a stable, multi-tasking, multi-user operating system for laptops, servers and desktops. Additionally, if you are a Windows user, you will be relieved to learn that UNIX has a GUI (graphical user interface) similar to the working environment of Microsoft Windows, which makes it easier for users to navigate and use. However, it is important to note that in this GUI, there are operations that are out of reach. Therefore, knowledge of UNIX use is necessary to operate commands and operations not covered by the GUI or in some instances, such as a Telnet session when the GUI interface is unavailable. I know you are getting lost in all the technical jargon and that's not the intention. To get a better understanding of Linux and, in effect, UNIX, let us go back in time to the circumstances that led to the birth of this Operating System.

### In our time machines

The year is 1960 something... Afro hairstyles and bell-bottom trousers are the "in" thing. Computers are the preserve of big tech companies and, to make it worse, they are as big as Noah's ark. Despite their size, this is by no means the most pressing problem that the then "geeks" were battling. Each computer had a different operating system. This means that, unlike today when you can own different computers all running the same system, each computer had to have its own operating system to serve a specific function or purpose. Think of it like this; if it were in today's setting, you would need one computer to type on and another computer to watch movies on. To top it off, being an expert in one system did not automatically mean that you were an expert in all the other systems. It was in these difficult and tumultuous times that scientists from Bell Labs decided that enough was enough. In 1969, they decided to develop a new operating system that was three things:

- Elegant and simple.

- Written in another computer language called C programming rather than the commonly used assembly code.

- A system that could be able to recycle the code generated.

After the development stages, the Bell scientists decided to name their brainchild "UNIX." UNIX was a "mass mover" mainly because it was the only system able to recycle code, unlike the other systems developed for one system. At that time, UNIX needed one piece of the special code i.e. the kernel, which was its popular name.

The kernel is the base of the UNIX system and is the piece of code needed to adapt to specific computers and function. In essence, what UNIX did was revolutionize things as they were then. The operating systems and all other functionalities of a computer were written in C language around the kernel. You are probably wondering, "Where did the Bell scientists get the C language from?" Well, they created it specifically for the UNIX system. The language (the C language) proved to be more flexible and could allow the creation of operating systems that could run on different hardware. It is important to note that in its early days, UNIX was not so much a home system and was thus used in big organizations with mainframes and mini computers such those used in the then

# Linux for Beginners

government and university environment. It was also in this environment that smaller computers were developed. In this stage of development, there were several versions of UNIX available but they were very slow and not really free; this led to the increase in use of the MS DOS on home computers.

We fast-forward to the 1990s when the computers got powerful enough to run a full UNIX system. A young man called Linus Torvalds was studying computer science at the University of Helsinki, and he thought to himself,

*"Hmm... would it not be nice if there was a free academic version of the UNIX?"*

Being a computer science student, and an inquisitive one at that, he started coding and asking many questions on UNIX. Most of the questions he asked revolved around being able to get the UNIX system running on his PC. There was much correspondences between him and the group called net landers but the one that may capture your attention is the one below posted in "comp.os.minix" in 1991.

```
From: torvalds@klaava.Helsinki.FI (Linus Bene-
dict Torvalds)
Newsgroups: comp.os.minix
Subject: Gcc-1.40 and a posix-question
Message-ID:
<1991Jul3.100050.9886@klaava.Helsinki.FI>
Date: 3 Jul 91 10:00:50 GMT
Hello netlanders,
Due to a project I'm working on (in minix), I'm
interested in the posix
standard definition. Could somebody please
point me to a (preferably)
machine-readable format of the latest posix
rules? Ftp-sites would be
nice.
```

From the correspondence, we can see that, from the beginning, it was Linus' goal to create a system compliant with the original UNIX but free. We can tell this by the fact that he asked for the POSIX standards, with POSIX being the standard for UNIX.

# Linux for Beginners

Back in those days, plug and play was not yet invented. However, this did not stop many people from showing a keen interest in owning and operating the UNIX system. What Linux is today is thanks to the people back then who were very keen on making sure that every new driver available for new hardware was submitted to the Linux test. This ended up causing a release of new codes at an amazing speed.

Now that we have looked at the somewhat unexpected birth of Linux, it is about time we got down to the inner workings of this operating system.

# Getting Started With the System

L inux is a mammoth operating system that derives its development from the millions of developers working on improving the open software. Because we cannot touch on everything, we shall start with some of the basic commands and work toward explaining the hard stuff. By getting into these basics, I assume that you have a Linux operating system. To log into the Linux system, you will require a username and password that you will use to log into the graphical user interface. The Linux system has two main modes of operation i.e. the sober-quick in text console mode which looks like a DOS operating system with a multi-tasking, multi-user and system that can be used with a mouse. The other mode is the graphical mode, which uses more system resources but looks and feels much better. Nowadays, the graphical mode is the most common in home computers. To know if you are logging into the graphic interface, you will be required to provide a username and password in two windows.

Perhaps I should also point to be careful when you are logging in with your account. Generally, it is not wise to log in using the root account (username). The root account is what most of us refer to as the administrator account. The reason for this is that the root account gives you the options of running extra programs with many special permissions. Therefore, to keep the risk of damaging the source code at a bare minimum, I suggest that you log in using your user account and only log in using the root account when you require more permission to execute a command.

To continue, you need to call up the terminal window or Xterm. X is the name of the software supporting the graphical environment. Finding the terminal will depend on the window manager you are using. However, to navigate to it, go to Application>Utilities-Internet menu or system tools (depending on your windows manager). Alternatively, you can access the Xterm by right clicking on the desktop. Because I want you to become a power user, the old point and click method will not do here. You will have to get down and dirty and meddle with the core of the system, which is what you will learn in subsequent chapters. Most of the advanced commands have to run through the shell, which we conjured up in the

# Linux for Beginners

terminal window we just learned how to access. If you are a Windows user looking to learn Linux for networking or system administration purposes, think of the terminal windows as your control panel. When you open the terminal window, it should always show a command prompt (akin to the C command in windows).

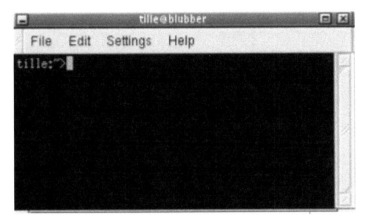

In the above instance, the terminal window displays the username and working directory represented by (~).

# Linux for Beginners

## Basic Linux commands

For your use, both in the graphical and text mode, I will provide you with a list of some of the most common commands. Some of these are quick start commands, and a link to more advanced commands at the end of these brief command sub topics.

| Command | Meaning |
|---|---|
| ls | This command displays a list of files in the working directory (current working directory for example the *dir* command in the DOS) |
| cd directory | Change directories |
| passwd | Means change the password for the current user |
| file filename | This displays the file types with the name filename |
| cat textfile | This throws the content of the textfile onto the screen |
| pwd | This command displays the current working directory |
| exit/logout | Executes a session leave |
| man command | This command reads the man pages on command |
| info command | Reads info pages on command |
| apropos string | Searches the *whatis database for strings* |

## The Linux files system

The files and systems in the Linux operating system are where most users find difficulties, mostly because it is hard to tell which files are in which directories if you do not have the knowledge. For this reason, we shall try to look at the organization of the file systems. We shall also learn how to create, delete, move and rename directories. Additionally, we will learn how to edit files and change permissions.

## The file system layout

The UNIX file system can aptly fit into a one-line description; "Everything on a UNIX system that is not a process is a file." This statement holds true for files that are a little bit more than just files (pipe and sockets that we shall look at shortly). Therefore, a Linux system does not differentiate between a file and directory mainly because the directory is, in essence, a file containing names of other files, services, texts, images and programs. Additionally, a Linux system also treats input and output devices as files. The general understanding is that the files are a sort of "in a tree" structure on the main hard drive; this is for easy management and order. Most of the files on a Linux system are regular files regardless of the data they hold, whether the files are programs, executable files or normal data.

While we have already said that everything in a Linux system is a file, there is a general understanding that there are some exceptions. For instance:

*Directories*: A file list of other files

*Special files*: These are the mechanisms used for input and output. Special files are in /dev.

*Links*: This is a system to make a file including directory visible in various parts of the "system tree."

*Domain (sockets)*: These are special types of files similar to the IP/TCP sockets. These files are protected by the file system access control and they provide inter process networking.

*Named pipes*: These types of files are the bridge between processes. They are more or less the same as sockets and enhance communication between processes without the use of networks or sockets semantics.

Remember that I had indicated that most computer users generalize that the file system is more or less like a tree, so here is a good example of a Linux file system tree.

# Linux for Beginners

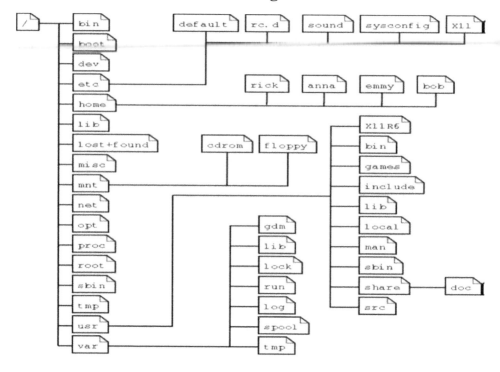

It is important to note that depending on the UNIX system in use, the file system tree may change; some files and directories may change.

The file system tree starts at the *slash* or the trunk, which, if you look at our table, is the (/) forward slash. This is what we call the root directory. It is the underlying directory for all files. Directories one level below the slash or root directory often have the slash in their proceeding names to indicate their position and to prevent confusion with other files or directories with similar names.

A question that plagues most Linux users is where programs and program files are stored when they are installed on the system. Let us examine this for a minute. Linux uses two partitions: The **data partition** where the system data, including the root directories and all system resources required to start the system are located, and the **swap partition**, which is an expansion of the physical memory on the computer. All files (including programs) are stored in this root directory in accordance to the Linux tree file system we have already looked at.

# Linux for Beginners

## Manipulating files

To show file names, properties, date of creation, permission, type, size, link files and owners, the **ls** command is the easiest way. As a Linux user, I suggest that you get acquainted with this command because you will use it often.

Creating and deleting files and directories on your system is very important when you want to create new files or delete redundant directories to free up space. Because the graphical interface is smaller or less complex than that of MS DOS, creating files is not that difficult. Deleting files on the other hand requires expertise to a moderately difficulty level. There are some popular file managers for the GNU/Linux, with most of them being executable files that are accessible from the desktop manager, home directory icon or the command line using the following commands.

## Managing files

*Nautilus*: This is the default file manager in the Gnome GNU desktop. There are very useful resources on how to use this tool online. How-to Geek is a good source of information.

*Konqueror*: This file manager is typical in KDE desktops. You can find a helpful usage handbook on Konqueror.org

Mc: Code named midnight commander is fashioned from the Norton commander. You can find some useful documentation on The Geek Stuff.com if you type the words "midnight commander Linux into your search.

For easier file management, the above applications are worth the time of reading through the documentation and the effort put in will really pay off. It is also important to note that there are many more file management applications; I have singled these ones out because they are the most popular and have a moderate difficulty level. Additionally, these tools optimize the UNIX commands in a specific manner. Let us examine how.

# Linux for Beginners

To keep files and things in one place, I suggest that you allocate specific files default locations by creating directories and sub directories for them. You can do this by using the **mkdir** command. For instance:

*john:~> mkdir archive*

*john:~> ls -ld archive*

*drwxrwxrwx 2 johnjohn 4096 Jan 13 14:09 archive/*

Additionally, you can create sub directories easily in one-step by using the –p option. For instance:

*john:~> cd archive*

*john:~/archive> mkdir 1999 2000 2001*

*john:~/archive>**ls***

*1999/ 2000/ 2001/*

*john:~/archive>**mkdir 2001/reports/Suppliers-Industrial/***

*mkdir: cannot create directory `2001/reports/Suppliers-Industrial/':*

*No such file or directory*

*john:~/archive>**mkdir -p 2001/reports/Suppliers-Industrial/***

*john:~/archive>**ls 2001/reports/***

*Suppliers-Industrial/:*

## File permissions

In some instances, you will find that the file needs more or other permissions not included in the file creation permission; this is what we call access right and is what we shall look at next.

Access rights are set using the same mkdir command. It is important to note that there are rules on how to name a directory. For instance, in one directory, you cannot have two files with the same name. However, it is

# Linux for Beginners

important to note that Linux, as well as UNIX, are case sensitive systems (you can have two file names with you and YOU in the same directory). Additionally, there are no limits (but not above 80 characters, which is almost a paragraph) to the length of a filename, so naming files should be a breeze. You can also use special characters in the file names as long as those characters do not hold a special meaning to the shell.

## Moving files

Moving unclassified files uses the mv command. Only attempt this after you have structured your home directory as we have done in the previous chapters of the book. If we use the same example above:

*john:~/archive> mv ../report[1-4].doc reports/Suppliers-Industrial/*

The command can also come in handy if you want to rename files:

*john:~> ls To_Do*
*-rw-rw-r-- 1 johnjohn 2534 May 15 11:40 To_Do*
*john:~> mv To_Do done*
*john:~> ls -l done*
*-rw-rw-r-- 1 johnjohn 2534 May 15 11:40 done*


In the above example, we can see that only the file name changes and all the other properties remain unchanged. When you encounter a problem in the command line, I suggest that you peruse the many help Linux forums available on the Internet or the info or main pages, as this is where most of the answers to system documentation are and are today treated as the how to and FAQ pages.

## Copying files

The cp command is used to copy directories and files. There is also a very useful option of copying all underlying subdirectories and files (recursive copy) which uses the –R. Here is a look at the general syntax.

cp [-R] fromfile tofile

# Linux for Beginners

## Removing or deleting files

The command rm comes in play when you want to remove single files, while the command rmdir plays its role in removing empty directories. It is important to note that some directories cannot be deleted (.dot and ..dot dot) because they are necessary for the proper ranking of a directory in the tree hierarchy. Like UNIX, Linux does not have a garbage can (recycle bin) and once you remove a file, it's permanent. It is gone and you cannot get it back unless you had a backup. To protect against this sometimes "mistaken delete", you can activate the interactive behavior of the cp, mv, and rm commands by using the -i option. When the –i option is active, the system does not execute command such as delete immediately; instead, it prompts for confirmation, which needs that stroke of a key or an additional click to execute the command fully. For instance:

*john:~> rm -ri archive/*

*rm: descend into directory `archive'? y*

*rm: descend into directory `archive/reports'? y*

*rm: remove directory `archive/reports'? y*

*rm: descend into directory `archive/backup'? y*

*rm: remove `archive/backup/sysbup200112.tar'? y*

*rm: remove directory `archive/backup'? y*

*rm: remove directory `archive'? y*

# How to Use Linux

In order to get started with the program Linux, it is important to know the steps to take. You are not going to be able to go on the system, and always have a way to learn all of the steps. This chapter is going to take some time to explain the steps that are necessary in order to get yourself started

## Familiarize Yourself with the System

The first thing that you are going to want to do with this program is to download it and make sure that it is completely installed onto your computer. Then you can go through and make sure that everything is working in the proper manner. If you are not sure if you will like this system, you should be aware that you will be able to keep up with the current operating system that you have while also dedicating a part of the hard drive of your computer to Linux. With the help of VirtualBox you could even run both of them at the same time to see how they work together side by side. You will then be able to learn how to use the program and decide if it is the setup that you like and how it all works.

## Test the Hardware using a Live CD

Many of the distributors of the Linux System are going to be able to provide you with an actual CD so that you will be able to try out the product without it having to be downloaded onto your computer. This is a great way to ensure that your hardware and all of the programs that you have on the computer are going to work well with this operating system before you have to download it. This can be really great because some people are going to feel uncomfortable with having to install a second kind of operating system onto their computer. With this live CD you will be able to boot up the Linux system straight from the CD without having to add anything or download it to the computer. There are also some other distributions of the Linux system, such as Ubuntu, that are going to offer a CD or a DVD that is going to allow you to boot up this system, use it for a while to see how well it is going to work with your hardware and your computer, and then you will be able to install it straight from the disk without having to go through any other steps along the way.

## Do Your Typical Computer Tasks

Once you have got Linux updated and put onto your computer, or you are using the CD, you should take the time to use some of the regular tasks that you would do on your normal operating system. These steps are going to be a little bit different for each person who is on the system based upon what they use the computer for. Take a minute to think: what are some of the things that you do on the computer on a normal day? What are some of the tasks that you might not do every day but which you do often enough that it matters, whether it is going to work or not. If you find that you are not able to find some solutions to tasks that you do, such as burn a CD or work on a word processing program that you have on your computer, you should make a note of it. Try to be as detailed as you are able to and make notes as you go. When you are done, you should be able to determine all of the things that you want to do, are able to do, and the things that you cannot do before you take the plunge with this Linux system. This is going to give you a good idea if the system is the right one for your needs and if you are going to still be able to get everything done or if there is going to be too much difficulty.

## Learn the Linux Distributions

When you are talking about the Linux distributions, it is more than likely going to refer to the GNU/Linux Distribution. This kind of distribution is a software collection that runs on top of the small program that is known as the Linux kernel. The kind of distribution that you will find in your program is going to determine the things that you are able to do and if the program is going to work with your computer. If you are unsure about how all of this works, it might be helpful to find someone who is able to assist you with the more technical aspects of this system.

## Think about doing a dual booting

This is a good thing to try out when you are first starting out on this system because it is going to allow you to still use your Windows platform while learning how to use the Linux system. One of the reasons that many are not going to switch over to the Linux program is because they are comfortable with their Windows program and are worried that they are going to mess things up if they do not like the Linux system or that they will not be able to get their Windows system back. The nice thing about Linux is that you are going to be able to run it right alongside of your Windows system. This is going to help you to learn how to partition the program while still using the system that you are used to. If you do not like the new system or you still want to be able to use your Windows system, it is possible to go back and forth between them the whole time that you are using the Linux system (at least until you decide to get rid of the Windows system and run solely on the Linux system). It is important that you take time to back up all of the personal data and the settings that you have on your computer before you try to do a dual boot or else you might find that you are going to lose things in the process.

## Install the Software

Once you have had time to experiment with the software on your system a little bit and figure out how to use it, if it is going to work well for your computer, and if you like it, it is time to start installing the software. You should get used to the installing and then the uninstalling software processes early on. This is important since understanding the management of the package and the repositories is one of the best ways that you are going to be able to understand the fundments of the Linux system. Once you are able to understand the system, it is a good idea to go through and install all of the software on your computer. If you are going to keep the old Windows software, this will be the last step that you need to do during the installing process. On the other hand, if you are going to get rid of the Windows system and just use Linux instead, you will be able to uninstall it once you have the Linux system fully updated and installed on your computer.

## Learn how to use along with enjoy the command interface

This system is known under several different names such as the shell, terminal window, or the terminal. This is one of the primary reasons that so many people are going to switch over to use Linux; the terminal is a great feature so it is important to learn how to enjoy and use it so that you do not become intimidated. It is one of your best allies that does not

# Linux for Beginners

include the same kind of limitations that you are going to find on the Windows command prompt. If you do not think that you are going to use the interface, you will still be able to get a lot of benefits out of the Linux system just like you would on a MAC OSX. Using apropos is also able to help you find the command that does each specific task. For example, if you type in apropos user, you will be able to see a long list of commands that have the word of user in their description and you will be able to see all of the great options that are available in your system.

## Learn the Linux System

Once all of the software is uploaded on your computer, you should take the time that is needed in order to learn about and get familiar with your file system. The first thing that you might notice when you are using this system is that there is no longer the C:\ like you would have seen in your Windows operating system. Everything in this system is going to starts at the root of the file system and the different kinds of hard drives that you will get to are going to be accessed through the /dev directory instead. The home directory, which would be like the C:\Documuents and through the settings on Windows XP and Windows 200o, is going to be found in /home with the Linux system. This is going to take you a little bit of work in order to get used to it, but once you do it is pretty easy to use.

## Continue to Investigate the Linux Install

There are many different things that you are going to be able to do with the Linux system and many of them you might not have realized when you were first getting started and looking it over. You can try out the encrypted partitions as well as the new and extremely fast file system, the redundant parallel disks that are going to be able to increase both the speed and the reliability of your system, and then you can try to install the Linux system to a bootable USB stick. It is not going to take long for you to discover that there are many things that you will be able to do with this system and you just need to take the time to learn about it all.

# Digging In- More Advanced Functions and Commands

## Using the shell features

In a previous chapter, (moving files) we looked at using the shell feature to manipulate multiple files in one instance. In the example, the shell automatically found out what the user (you) meant by the requirements between the square braces "[" "]". Coincidentally, the shell can substitute a range of numbers, lower and upper case characters, and as many characters as you want with an asterisk. You can use many substitutions simultaneously because the shell handles these substitutions very logically. For instance, the bash shell finds no problems with expressions such as the ls dirname/*/*/*[2-3]. However, in other shells, we use the asterisk to minimize the efforts of typing. For instance, instead of entering cd directory, you enter cd dir*. In the Bash GNU, this not necessary because the shell has a feature called file name completion which makes it possible to type the first few characters of a command and the shell finds what you are looking for. For instance, in a directory full of files, you can search for files beginning with the letter A by typing Is A and double pressing the tab key rather than the enter key.

## Looking up files

The simplest way to search for files is by using the *which*command to search for directories indexed in the user search path. The path only contains files or directories containing executable files or programs, which makes the "which" command redundant. The "which" command is especially convenient when diagnosing "command not found". Let us look at an example where our user "john" cannot use the acroread program, while a colleague of his has no problems with the program on the same system. The colleague tells John that he can see the program in */opt/acroread/bin* but the directory is not in the path:

*john:~>which acroread /usr/bin/which: no acroread in (/bin:/usr/bin:/usr/bin/X11).*

We can solve this problem by commanding the full path to run. Alternatively, we can re-export the content of the variable path:

*john:~> export PATH=$PATH:/opt/acroread/bin*

*tina:~> echo $PATH*

*/bin:/usr/bin:/usr/bin/X11:/opt/acroread/bin*

The command (the which command) also checks whether the command is an alias for another command:

*gerrit:~> which -a ls*

*ls is aliased to `ls -F --color=auto'*

*ls is /bin/ls*

If the above command does not work, I suggest that you use the alias command

*tille@www:~/mail$ alias ls*

*alias ls='ls --color'*

## Finding and locating files

The find tool is the real tool to use when searching for directories that are not in the path. It is a very powerful tool, but most users consider it a somewhat difficult syntax. The GNU find, on the other hand, handles syntax problems. The command allows you to search file names and access file sizes, dates of change and almost all the other file property changes.

*find <path> -name <searchstring>*

This means look in all subdirectories and files in the specified path and print a list of all the files with a name in the search criteria (string name and not the content) you can use the search command to search for files of a certain size. For example, let us assume our user john wants to find files larger than 5mb:

*john:~> find . -size +5000k*

*psychotic_chaos.mp3*

# Trotting in the Mud...Getting Deeper

## Using text editors

The first step to independence on your system is learning how to use a text editor. Text editors are especially useful to the advanced user who wants to write scripts, new programs and build websites. A text editor is a productivity tool that will help you greatly. The text editors are usable both in graphical environment and in a terminal window. Additionally, mastering the text editor will allow you to use it on remote machines, which improves network speeds tremendously. Below are the most common editors.

## Gnu Emacs

Emacs is very popular on almost all UNIX based systems. It is extensible, self-documenting, customizable and the best real time display editor. It automatically updates the text edited on the screen as you type your command. What makes it real time is the fact that the display is in a constant state of update, at the stroke of each character. Most users refer to it as an advanced editor because it goes beyond providing the facilities of simple deletion and insertion. It can express comments in several programming languages, automate indentation of programs, control sub processes, edit formatted text, view multiple files at the same time etc. It is self-documenting, meaning that once you type any special character for example Ctrl+H, you can use it to find out the actions of the command or all topics pertaining to that topic.

## Vim

Vim is an acronym for "Vi Improved". It was previously "VIimitation". The text editor contains almost all the commands in the UNIX command line and then some more. To enter commands in the Vim editor, you have to use a keyboard. Learning to use this text editor will be an advantage because it is the most common editor on all UNIX systems. It is also ideal for the beginner user because of the in-built menu help.

# Linux for Beginners

## SSH keys

To generate, convert, manage, and generate Ssh keys, you can use the ssh-keygen command. An Ssh key is a way of identifying trusted computers without using passwords. The ssh-keygen can create RSA usable on the Ssh protocol, version 1 and more.

## Using Cron to schedule jobs

The most standard way to run tasks in the background is to use cron jobs. The program is valuable in automating tasks related to the machine such as maintenance. Cron is a background daemon program. The tasks scheduled run in a configuration file called cron tab.

Most of the distros have one form of cron preinstalled at default. However, in those instances where your distro does not have the cron installed, here is how you do it.

### For Ubuntu/Debian:

sudo apt-get update

sudo apt-get install cron


### For Cent OS/Red Hat Linux:

*sudo yum update*

*sudo yum install vixie-cron crontabs*


Here is how to activate its background functions.

*sudo /sbin/chkconfig crond on*

*sudo /sbin/service crond start*

# Linux for Beginners

For example, here is a task we want to run

*5 * * * * curl http://www.google.com*

While the syntax for the jobs we place on the crontab may at first glance look intimidating, they are actually an easy-to-parse, succinct way of reading it if you know how to. Most of the commands (or each command) are broken into two:

*Schedule*

*Command*

The command is any task, or otherwise, you would execute on the command line. On the other hand, the schedule part of the syntax is in five different options that you can use to schedule. They are in the following order:

**MIN** HOUR **DOM** MON **DOW** CMD

Table: Crontab Fields and Allowed Ranges (Linux Crontab Syntax)

| Field | Description | Allowed Value |
|---|---|---|
| MIN | Minute field | 0 to 59 |
| HOUR | Hour field | 0 to 23 |
| DOM | Day of Month | 31-Jan |
| MON | Month field | 12-Jan |
| DOW | Day Of Week | 0-6 |
| CMD | Command | Any command to be executed. |

Here are a few examples to give you a clearer picture of what we mean; you will encounter some of them as you work to configure cron.

*To run a per minute command*

\* \* \* \* \*

Here is how to run a command every 12th minute of each hour

*12 \* \* \* \**

If you want to run a command every 15 minutes, you can use placeholders for different options.

*0,15,30,45 \* \* \* \**

For running a command at 4 am every day, you would need to use

*0 4 \* \* \**

On the other hand, to run a command at 4 am every Tuesday, this is what you use

*0 4 \* \* 2*

You can also use division in the schedule. How so? For instance, instead of using /listing 0, 15, 30, 45, you can substitute it with this

*\*/4 2-6 \* \* \**

In the above range, the syntax will execute a command between 2-6 am.

Think of the scheduling syntax as your all-powerful magic wand that you can use for expression at any time you can imagine.

## Configuration

After you have decided what to run at a specific time (schedule), you have to place it in a place that makes it easier for your daemon to discover it for reading. Even though there are a few places to place it, the user crontab is the most common. The crontab is the file that holds a schedule of jobs on cron. Each user has their own file located at *var/spool/cron/crontab*; the file should not be edited directly. To edit, use the crontab command. Here is the command that you require:

*crontab –e*

The above command calls up the text editor. You can use the text editor to input your job schedule. Each job should be on a new line. If you would like to view your crontab without editing it, use the command below:

*crontab -l*

Below is the command to erase the crontab

*crontab –r*

If you are a user with all the privileges of an admin, here is how you edit another user

*crontab -u <user> -e*

## Output

Unless you direct the output for every job executed into a log file, the output is sent via email to the user email attached to the cron job executed. Fortunately, you can specify which email to send the log file to by providing a "'mailto" in the setting option at the top of the crontab. Additionally, you can specify which shell to run, home directory, and the cron binary search path by following the examples below.

Let us start by editing the crontab

*crontab –e*

This is how you can edit it.

*SHELL=/bin/bash*

*HOME=/*

*MAILTO="example@example.com"*

*#This is a comment*

*\* \* \* \* \* echo 'Run this command every minute'*

According to everything we have learnt so far, we know that this job will have the output of "execute (run) this command every minute". Because we have specified the email "example@example.com, the log file will be sent every minute to the email we have specified. This does not sound like an ideal situation (unless you want thousands of log files in your mail inbox). The better option would be to pipe the output file into an empty location.

Here is how you append a log file

*\* \* \* \* \* echo 'Run this command every minute' >> file.log*

An important factor to note here is that ">>" appends the file

To pipe the file into an empty location, you can use */dev/null.*

For example, this PHP script is executed and runs in the background

*\* \* \* \* \* /usr/bin/php /var/www/domain.com/backup.php > /dev/null 2>&1*

## Restricting access

You can also restrict access with cron in an easy way by using */etc/cron.allow* and */etc/cron.deny.*

To restrict or allow a user, you simply need to place their username in the user file, which is dependent on the access granted. The default settings in cron daemon assumes that all users can access cron i.e. unless the access files exist. For example, to give access to the user john and deny access to all other users, this is the command you would use.

*echo ALL >>/etc/cron.deny*

*echo john >>/etc/cron.allow*

By using the appendix "ALL", we lock out and deny all users access to the file. On the other hand, we give the user access to execute jobs by appending the username.

## Special syntax

If all the cron commands that we have looked at so far seem very hard, there are shorthand commands you can use to make your administration easier. Think of them as shortcuts.

*@hourly - Shorthand for 0 \* \* \* \**

*@daily - Shorthand for 0 0 \* \* \**

*@weekly - Shorthand for 0 0 \* \* 0*

*@monthly - Shorthand for 0 0 1 \* \**

*@yearly - Shorthand for 0 0 1 1 \**

Additionally, you can use *@reboot,* to run a command once at startup.

It is important to note that not all the cron daemons can construe this syntax and you should check for that before you rely on their operation.

In addition to that which we have looked at, you can also have a job run at startup by editing your crontab file *crontab –e*and placing a line similar to the one below:

*@reboot echo "System start up"*

# Choosing a Distro- Which Way to Go

A distro is a specific GNU/Linux operating system vendor package. Additionally, a distro can also be a set of open source components and software assembled together. In the Linux user community, there is a raging debate as to which distro is the best. The arguments are biased between which distro is the best for first timers and new users. To get a better picture, we shall set aside all the bias and look at it from an analytical point of view. However, it is important to note that even with a critical point of view, it is almost impossible to point out a specific distro as the best because the one you or someone else chooses is dependent on their needs. Our analysis is on the distro usability (ease of use) and the look and feel of the user interface (design). The distros we shall look at are on this list because they meet the following criteria.

*1 Is user friendly

*2 Has out of the box apps

*3 Has an app store in one form of the other

*4 Has a user interface that is somewhat modern and up to date

Let us look at each criteria in-depth.

## User friendly

This is the most critical factor we have to consider. Imagine you are a user who just downloaded a distro; you install it into your hardware in the hopes of using it only to find that it is more or less like mathematical algorithms that require a physics or mathematical PhD to decipher. An ideal distro must be like noodles, easy to make, i.e. easy to use. If you require a big rocket science manual to navigate through a distro, it fails the user-friendly test. The major reason why a distro must be user-friendly is because most users are accustomed to simply sitting at a Windows or OS

# Linux for Beginners

X desktop and commence use immediately. Making a distro hard to use, it is extremely unlikely that anyone will use it frequently or even like it.

## Out of the box apps

Let us look at a simple scenario. You download and install a distro, try to check your email inbox, only to find that the distro does not have an email client. Therefore, you decide to do it online, you search for the web browser only to come up void. You then decide to use your mobile device to check your email and listen to some music from your computer as you do that, and there is no music player. For a distro to be on our list of potentials, it must have the above features or apps pre-installed. The list of these out of the box distros grows shorter and shorter each year and you might want to check each distro for your specific out of the box app needs.

## Application store

Adding an application to a Linux operating system is no mean feat. Here is where an app store comes in. If you consider the fact that most users today are accustomed to easy to install applications on their mobile devices, it makes sense that a distro without an inbuilt app store will not be a favorite. One of the oldest app stores is synaptic. App stores make it easier for users to add software to the environment.

## Interface

If you take any modern device today, be it a mobile phone, smart TV, game console and any other, you will notice that all of these devices have a very modern UI (user interface). Users are very fond of the swank UI and the desktop is no exception. A distro must be enticing to the user. It must have an easy to use, but unique, interface. In fact, today, most users choose a distro by checking the user interface.

# Linux for Beginners

## Top Three Distros

With the criteria above in mind, let us examine some of the three top distros. It is also important to note that the distros made it to the list only because they pass all our tests.

## Ubuntu

If we were to take a critical approach at Ubuntu Linux, we would say that it is and has been "the king" of the user-friendly kingdom. In my view, User-friendly on this distro is as easy as they come. It is intuitive and logical. Ubuntu unity, the most powerful search tool on an UNIX desktop also comes as an add-on to this distro.

## Linux mint

If Ubuntu Linux is the king of all distros, Linux mint is the prince. Because it is a variation of Ubuntu (based on it), it benefits greatly from the reliability and stability, but with a more eye candy approach. Unlike Ubuntu Linux, the Linux mint takes a more standard approach to the desktop and that is what makes it stand out in the desktop metaphor.

## Linux Deepin

This is a relatively new distro from China. It takes the powerful Linux desktop and transforms it into artistic beauty, but with the same level of user-friendly features. If you have heard of the GNOME 3 desktop, Linux Deepin is a completely awesome and marvelous retool of it.

Now that we have listed three of the top contenders for the best distro, let us check each to our criteria and give each of the distro a score and rank. We shall call this scoring. We shall rank from first to last using the criteria we have discussed and then total them all to see which one comes out top with the winner being the distro with the lowest score.

## Scoring the distros

### User-friendly

The user-friendliness of a distro depends on the user, so it is a bit hard to say which one is the best. Additionally, my best may not be your best, so look at all of them, and make a sound decision on the one that suits your sense of style. Here is how they rank:

*1 Linux Mint

*2 Ubuntu Linux

*3 Linux Deepin

Why does the mint make it to the top? The mint has the taskbar, start menu and desktop icons and an almost zero learning curve. However, it is important to note that both Linux Deepin and Ubuntu also have an almost zero learning curve so the Mint barely made it to the top on this one.

### Common apps

All our three distros have the prerequisite apps and this makes it extremely hard to be a judge in this category. However, it is important to note that Linux Deepin comes with the finest office suite solution: the Kingsoft Office, which they (the developers) hope to change to LibreOffice this year (2014). Each of the distro has a default music player as below:

*Linux Deepen-Dmusic

*Ubuntu- Rhythm Box

*Linux Mint- Banshee

# Linux for Beginners

Out of the three music players, Banshee has the most features. For the best interface, Dmusic is your choice. Moreover, if you are looking for reliability, Rhythm Box is your best choice.

If we were to score them, this is how they would rank:

*1 Linux Mint

*2 Ubuntu Linux

*3 Linux Deepin


## App store

For a new user, an app store can make them a continuous user or a sour bad-review spitting user. Therefore, the app store has to be one of the criteria we use to rank our distros. Each of our three distros has its own approach to the app store as follows:

*Linux Deepin- Deepin Software Center

*Mint- Software manager

*Ubuntu- Ubuntu Software Center

All the app stores have the Ubuntu Software Center as their backbone. This sounds a bit odd, but the reason why the software center falls at tail end of our list is that it is extremely slow regardless of the computing power of your hardware.

Here is how we would rank them:

*1 Linux Deepin

*2 Linux mint

*3 Ubuntu Linux

# Linux for Beginners

While the app stores function in an almost similar manner, there are two reasons why Deepin made it to the top. It has an easy to use and navigate interface and it loads up faster than the other two.

## Modern UI

When it comes to the category of user interface, it is safe to say that Linux mint is not a contender. The desktop is a bit outdated and even on a computer with very powerful graphics, the desktop still looks like a Mac one from the 1990s. This is not to say that the desktop is not appealing. In the interface category, this is how the distros rank:

*1 Linux Deepin

*2 Ubuntu Linux

*3 Linux Mint

Linux Deepin makes it to the top of the list because it uses GNOME 3 to generate a combination of the GNOME and the OS X to make an attractive interface that makes you feel as if you are looking at a beautiful piece of art.

Although it is a bit rudimentary and biased towards my overall outlook that is dependent on my needs, this is how the distros rank overall.

*1 Linux Mint has a collective score of 7 out of 10

*2 Linux Deepin has a collective score of 8 out of 10

*3 Ubuntu Linux has a score of 9 out of 10


For new users, Linux mint is the best choice. However, most of the distros we have looked at are top notch and you cannot go wrong with any of them. If you are one of those people who love artistic desktops, Linux Deepin is the best choice. If you want to strike a balance between ease of use and beauty, Ubuntu Linux is your best pick. When you are looking for simple without the artistic desktop or interface, then Linux mint is your best choice. Choosing a distro will largely depend on your needs and preference.

# Setting up Linux on Windows and Mac

## Connecting to Linux from Mac and Windows computers

Connecting to Linux via Windows or OS x computers requires the installation of special software. In is chapter, we shall look at the various ways by which you can do that.

### Connecting to Linux server via Windows using Putty

By using Putty, you can form a secure connection to your Linux server from a Windows computer. Putty is a free SSH and Telnet implementation software for UNIX and Windows platforms. We shall use this tool to create a connection.

Head over to the Putty website and ensure that you read through and agree with the license agreement. After the download, launch the application. The next step is to configure your connections.

### Configuring your connection

After launching the application, head over to the PUTTY configuration window and enter the following values and open.

*Enter your cloud server IP address on the host name*

### Be sure to set the connection type to SSH

Optionally, you can give your connection a name by clicking the saved session field. You can use any name of your choosing because it is a time

# Linux for Beginners

saving measure for the next time you launch PUTTY. Additionally, you can assign different names to your cloud servers

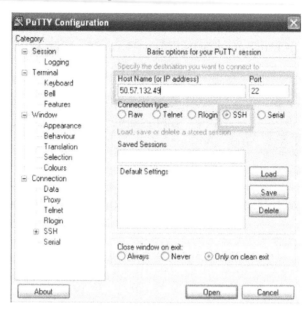

If you have never used PUTTY to log into your server with SSH before, there will be a pop up warning similar to the one in the figure below.

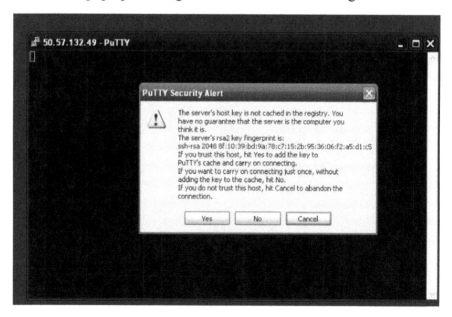

# Linux for Beginners

If you are not sure of the information entered, press no and recheck the information, otherwise press yes. This pop up is a one-time verification and subsequent connections will not prompt for it because Windows will add the host key to your registry. However, if you connect to that server from another computer or install a fresh copy of the operating system on your computer, the figure above will pop up.

## Enter your password and username

After clicking yes on the warning pop up, the terminal will prompt for your password and username (not in that order). If you have never logged onto the server, make sure to use the root user to log in. If the terminal prompts for the password to the root user, enter the password for the current root user. After entering the password, you have to press enter because the password prompt does echo on the screen. If your password is correct, the response will be a shell prompt:

*[root@yourservername ~]#*

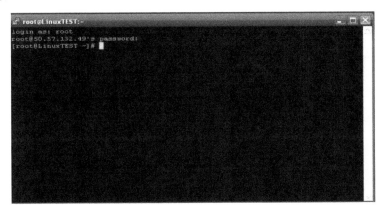

This will allow you access to your server with all permissions granted. Like most accounts, I recommend that you change your root account password to something cryptic and personal. Performing this is possible by using the passwd command. This is how you do it.

# Linux for Beginners

*1 Enter the password command from the shell prompt

*2 Type the new password that you want to use on your servers. Because the password does not echo on the screen, reenter the password and execute.

Type in the new password and press execute. This is your new password and you will use it with your root account whenever you connect to the server.

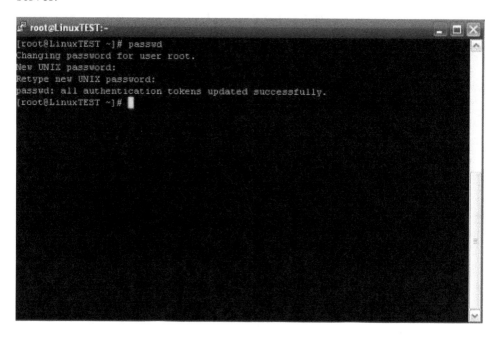

## Connecting to server via OS X

Unlike on Windows where you need to use third party software such as Putty to connect to your Linux server, in OS X, you do not need to install any client. Mac OSX has an inbuilt program, terminal, which is a terminal emulator. You can use this terminal to run SSH.

# Linux for Beginners

## How to connect to server

The following instructions are for first time cloud-server connections. When you are non-root user, use your username instead of root.

Step 1- Head over to applications >then Utilities and call up the terminal.

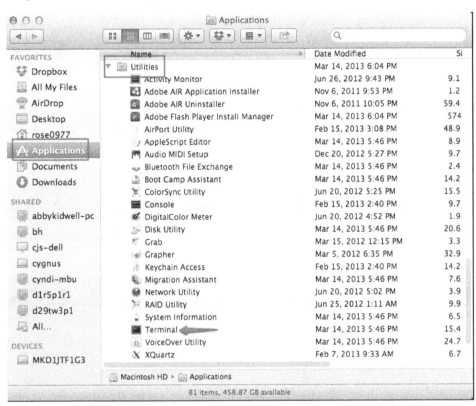

This is what the terminal window will display:

```
user00241 in ~MKD1JTF1G3->$
```

Use the following syntax to establish a SSH connection to the server:

```
ssh root@IPaddress
```

For instance

# Linux for Beginners

```
MKD1JTF1G3->$ ssh root@166.76.69.51
```

Because this is your first connection to your server and the RSA key is not yet in your system registry, you will get a message prompting for continuation confirmation.

```
The authenticity of host '198.61.208.131 (198.61.208.131)' can't be established.
RSA key fingerprint is 47:ff:76:b4:211:0f:11:15:21:bd:92:2f:44:0a:d9:0a.
Are you sure you want to continue connecting (yes/no)?
```

To add the RSA key to the trusted hosts, you need to press yes and execute. As is the windows setup we did earlier, this prompt will only appear once. Enter your server root password. It is important to note that the server is not echoed onto the screen.

```
MKD1JTF1G3-$ ssh root@198.61.208.131
root@198.61.208.131's password:
```

Unless you use the correct password, the shell prompt will not respond:

```
[root@yourservername ~]#
```

## How to change the password

After logging in for the very first time, it is advisable to change your root password. You can change the password by accessing the shell prompt and using this command.

```
passwd
```

Below is how you change the password, but it is not echoed onto the screen:

```
Enter new UNIX password:
Retype new UNIX password:
```

Make sure that the passwords match for the change to be successful. If they match, you will receive a notification (confirmation) of token authentication.

Passwd: password updated successfully

You will use this newly created password every time you log into your root user to connect to your server.

# Reasons to Use Linux`

There are many different programs that are out on the market that you can choose to use for your programming needs. All of them are going to have things that you are going to love and other things that you might not like as much. There is not going to be a program out there that is going to be everything that you ever wanted because everyone has their own preferences. If you have to pick one of the best programming software systems that you can get on the market, there is nothing that is better and has more benefits than that offered by Linux. This chapter is going to give you some of the best reasons why you should choose to go with the Linux system rather than choosing one of the other systems the market.

**Linux is free** — One of the reasons that you might want to look at using this program is that it is free. This is in fact one of the main benefits that people will look into when they are picking this product over others on the market. This is a great thing, especially if you are just learning how to do programming and you do not want invest a huge amount before seeing if you can get on with the program. If you are starting out with a programming career, you might find that having a free Linux system is a great benefit because you can keep your costs minimal. You will be able to use this product for however long you like and once you do, chances are that you won't look back.

**Easy to use and install this product**—It is not going to take a lot of time for you to download this product and you are going to be able to figure out how to use it in no time, no matter how much experience you have with this system. This means that it is a great product to use if you are a beginner with this kind of system because you are not going to need a lot of experience. You will then be able to get started on your work in no time without a lot of delays.

# Linux for Beginners

**Commercial support**—In the past, many businesses found that they were going to have trouble getting the commercial support that they needed in order to get the work done. This is one of the main reasons that they might have chosen to stay with Windows in the past. Canonical, Novell and Red Hat, the three big companies that provide Linux, have been able to put this fear to rest. This means that you will be able to get the commercial support that you need for this product whenever you need it. Each of the companies listed above offer support at any time of the day, all year long in order to help support your mission critical applications as well as the other business needs that you have.

**NET Support**—Businesses that have had to standardize this work on the Microsoft technology, especially when it comes to their .NET web technology, will be happy to find out that the Linux platform is going to be able to support all of these same applications. Novell owns and helps to support the Mono project that is set up to maintain the .NET compatibility that you are looking for. One of the goals of the Mono project is to be able to provide businesses with the ability that they need in order to make choices and to resist the lock-in that can happen to vendors. Additionally, this project is able to offer Visual Studio plugins so that the .NET developers are easily able to transfer their products from Windows without changing all of the work that they are doing or changing their familiar development tools. This effort is put in because the developers know that .Net application stability with Linux is much better than what can be found with Windows and so they want to be able to provide this service to all potential customers.

**Unix uptimes**—Linux stability is able to offer business owners the peace that they need to know that their applications are not going to go through long outages due to having issues with the stability of an operating system. Linux is going to enjoy some of the best uptimes because of their connection with Unix. This stability is able to prove that Linux is able to support you as much as any other program that is available. Rebooting after each patch, service pack, or any other changes can make a program unreliable which are things that you do not have to worry about when it comes to this system. You will be able to know that your design is going to be up and running at all of the times that you need it to be.

**Security**—When you are working on a platform like this, you are going to want to make sure that you have an operating system that is as secure as possible. Of course, you are not going to be able to find one that is going to be secure all of the time. But with Linux, you are going to get some of the best security that is on the market. From the updates to the daily lists of patches that are done, the Linux code is going to keep the system as secure as possible. The owners who are relying on the commercially supported Linux systems will be able to access all of the available security fixes that are offered. With this platform, you are going to have a community that is available throughout the world that can secure the fixes rather than having to rely on just one company that has a closed source code; when this happens you are dependent on the response that is coming from one company to get the fixes that you want, which is sometimes going to take a little bit of time to get done. When you have a program like Linux, many companies are going to work to provide you with the fixes that you need so that you can get taken care of right away.

Transferrable skills—one of the barriers that came up when Linux was first developed was that it was too different from Unix so that when administrators from Unix tried to move over to Linux, they would not be able to do it. The Linux layout looks a lot like any of the commercial versions of Unix and it also uses a lot of the standard commands that come with Unix. There are a few commands in Linux that are not able to transfer, but this is going to also be true when you are switching between versions of Unix. This means that those who are used to using Unix are going to be able to easily move over to Linux without any issues.

**Commodity hardware**—One of the things that many business owners like about the Linux software is that they are able to use their old systems, even the ones that are out of date, on Linux and it is still going to work well. Fortunately for those who are adopting Linux into their lives, there are no issues with hardware upgrades that are going to follow with each of the new versions of the software that is released. This means that when you get a new version, you are still going to be able to use some of the old programs that you have without having to worry about whether the program is going to work or not.

**Worldwide community**—Linux is great in that it provides you with a worldwide community of different developers that are going to contribute to the system enhancements, security fixes, and source code that help to make the system run. This community is also there to provide your business with some free support through different forums and other community sites. This kind of community is a great way to get the peace of mind that you need as a Linux user because there is not going to be just one single point where the failure occurs and no single source where the development and support are coming from.

**Linux foundation**—this is a corporate collective of many different platinum supporters such as Oracle, Novell, NEC, Intel, IBM, HP, Hitachi, and Fujitsu, and other members who, through memberships and donations dues, sponsor what is known as Linus Torvalds and the others who are working at Linux full time. The purpose of this foundation is to help standardize, protect, and promote Linux in order to help fuel the growth that is needed for it around the world. This foundation is the source of all the things that are considered Linux. This is a big positive for all Linux users and the adopters because it gives the assurance that Linux is going to be continually developed to get things done.

**Regular updates**—This product is going to provide you with updates on a regular basis so that you are not having to wait around for it like you were doing with the Windows service pack that takes 18 months to occur. With Linux you are able to get new and improved versions of the product every six months. Every distribution of Linux is able to offer regular updates of the sources and packages that it offers several times each year as well as any security fixes that are needed even if they are needed more than twice a year. You will be able to get rid of any of the angst that you are feeling about upgrading your system because the update and the upgrade is easy and you are not going to have to reboot the system when you are done.

 As you can see, there are a lot of different benefits that you will be able to get from using this system, especially when you are able to compare it to the other systems that are on the market. It is a great idea to take the time to look over this product if you would like one system that is going to work out the best to meet all of your needs without having to worry about security or ease of use that you might have had to do with the rest of your software.

# What Can I do Using Linux?

After you have downloaded the Linux system onto your computer, you will be bombarded with all of the cool new things that you are able to do with this operating system. . This chapter is going to talk about some of the projects that you are able to do with this great operating system. You may be surprised at its versatility.

## Host Photo Album

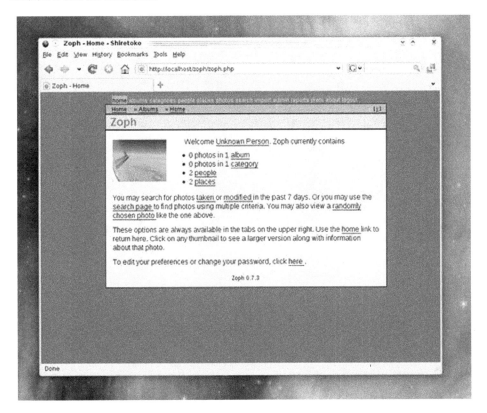

While there are many different online services that you can use in order to host a photo album, such as Picasa and Flickr, none of them are not the most ideal for helping you to share your personal photos with friends and family. Even when the other sites are going to offer collections with passwords and other restricted access, it is still not going to be as secure as hosting your own photo collection on your computer. Zoph is a program that is able to work well on Linux that is going to allow you to do just this. It is going to let you import your collection of photos either through a Tar or Zip file, organize them in the albums that you want, and then will set attributes for the author and the geographic region before letting your friends and family see them. This is a great way for you to show off your pictures to those that you love without having to worry about others getting ahold of them that do not need to.

## Build a Media Server

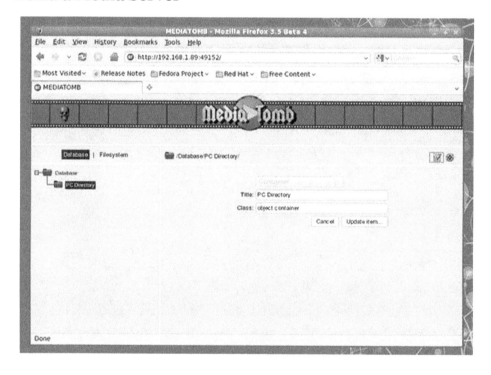

Linux is known for making brilliant serving files. The ability that comes from Linux is what keeps the enterprise world going to Linux for the heavy jobs and that helps the world use Google no matter what time of day it is. In addition, Linux is good at serving files that are tucked away from a computer and the server in your home is going to soon become an essential accessory for many different companies. Mobile phones, televisions, and games consoles are quickly developing the ability to play, display, and read files that are held on a media center PC and Linux is the perfect software that you can use to do this. All that you are going to need is a PC that is relatively low powered along with some good storage and a good place to keep it all. The best part is that you will be able to do all of this for free with the Linux system. This software is easy to download if you are using the Linux operating system through the Ubuntu server.

## Create Music

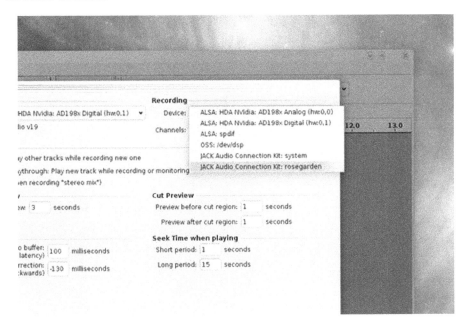

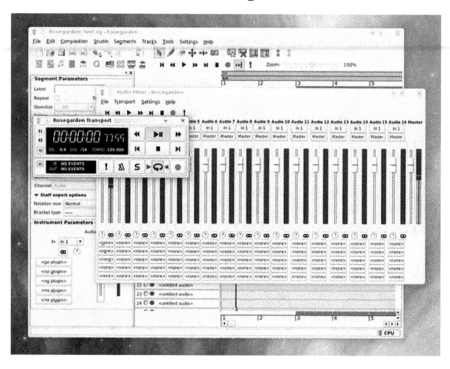

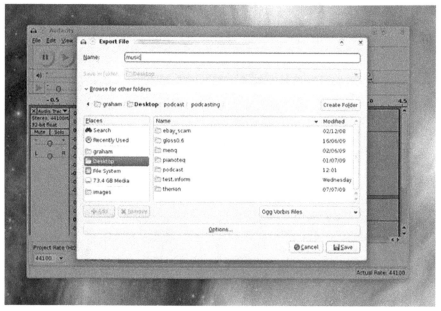

# Linux for Beginners

Everyone likes to be able to create something that is pleasant to the ear, whether they are just doing it for fun or they want to see if they are able to make it in the music business. It is not necessary that you have musical training in order to tell the difference between what music sounds good to you and what does not. With the Linux system you are going to be able to use the Rosegarden program that can help you create chords, melody and drum tracks through internal instruments before being able to save all of this to a file. In order to use this system, you will be using Rosegarden to communicate with your audio hardware along with the other audio applications. Make sure that you get all of the right software together in order to get started. You will then be able to get started with the bass track. Pick the first track number in the program and then the Track Parameters on the left in order to get the right sound. You can mix things together and have some fun in order to get the right sound that you are looking for.

## Write Interactive Fiction

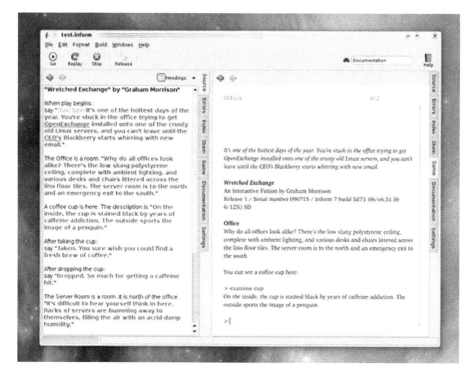

Have you ever wanted to be an author but wanted to try something that is a little bit different? The Linux system is going to be able to help you with this. Text adventure games were really fun and popular back when computers first started and they are beginning to gain some more popularity since mobile devices are being used more frequently. It is not necessary to be a coding guru in order to write your stories either since this is going to be made using a form of your natural language.

For example, the game is going to understand the relative positions and the names of the two locations that are described by the line "The library is west of the landing." This means that with the help of the Linux system you are going to be able to develop games and find out that it is almost as much fun as actually playing the games. In addition, there is going to be a great development environment that is going to help you in mapping out the locations and the ideas for the game as well as being able to help you understand and enter the source code in order to get your game to work out well. All you have to do is download the Gnome Inform onto your Linux and it is just that easy to get started.

# Conclusion

Once you get to using Linux like a pro, I can personally guarantee that you will never look back, or opt for any other system. The beauty of Linux (regardless of which distro you opt for) is the flexibility it affords you especially if you are a network administrator, app or system developer. I urge you to give it a whirl and enjoy the most amazing open source operating system available.

If you do make some amazing open source software or an app that you think could be beneficial to the millions of Distro users out there, do not hesitate to share it with others; that is the beauty of open source.

Thank you again for buying this book!

I hope this book was able to help you to learn how to use Linux command Line

The next step is to practice the command line as often as possible.

Finally, if you enjoyed this book, would you be kind enough to leave a review for this book on Amazon?

Thank you and good luck!


M.J. Brown

www.ingramcontent.com/pod-product-compliance
Lightning Source LLC
LaVergne TN
LVHW052314060326
832902LV00021B/3884